What Is
a Solar Eclipse?

What Is
a Solar Eclipse?

by Dana Meachen Rau

illustrated by Gregory Copeland

Penguin Workshop

To all the stargazers—DMR

PENGUIN WORKSHOP
An imprint of Penguin Random House LLC, New York

First published in the United States of America by Penguin Workshop,
an imprint of Penguin Random House LLC, New York, 2024

Visit us online at penguinrandomhouse.com.

Library of Congress Cataloging-in-Publication Data is available.

Printed in the United States of America

ISBN 9780593660911 (paperback)   10 9 8 7 6 5 4 3 2 1 WOR
ISBN 9780593660928 (library binding)   10 9 8 7 6 5 4 3 2 1 WOR

Contents

What Is a Solar Eclipse?

Kate Russo's life changed on August 11, 1999, while traveling in France. It was the first time she saw the sun disappear behind the moon. This total solar eclipse was such an amazing sight that Kate decided to spend her life studying, writing about, and chasing solar eclipses around the world.

The sun doesn't really disappear during a total solar eclipse. It just looks like it does. During a solar eclipse, the sun, moon, and earth line up, and the moon casts a shadow on a part of the earth. The dark round shape of the moon passes over the brightness of the sun. The sun seems to grow smaller until it is black, surrounded by a halo of light. On earth, everything in the shadow of the moon goes dark for a few minutes. Then, the sun begins to emerge as the moon moves away.

Solar eclipses happen often, but the chances of seeing an eclipse more than once in the same location occurs only every three hundred to four hundred years. And they are not always viewable over land. Sometimes eclipses can only be seen over the ocean or in areas where few people live. But that doesn't stop an eclipse chaser like Kate Russo, who once traveled by boat far into the Pacific Ocean just to see an eclipse. Eclipse

chasers are also known as umbraphiles (say: UM-bruh-files), which means "shadow lovers."

Scientists can predict when eclipses will happen. So umbraphiles know where and when to watch them. They plan trips to be in the right place at the right time to get the best view. They visit islands and climb up mountains. They go to the hot desert and the freezing Arctic. If an eclipse occurs over the ocean, they take cruise ships.

If bad weather is predicted, they take airplanes to see the sky from above the clouds.

Why are umbraphiles willing to travel so far for an experience that lasts only a few minutes? Because they like the way it makes them feel! Eclipse chasers have described watching these events as magical and mysterious, beautiful, powerful, and exciting. It gives them goose bumps. Umbraphiles may bring along special cameras and viewing equipment. But they also treat the eclipse as a celebration. People from all over the world meet up and share in the event. Some have traditions: One viewer always wears orange pants. Another brings a special flag. And another brings along the same teddy bear! The experience can be simply awesome.

You don't have to be an umbraphile to enjoy watching an eclipse. You might live close enough to the path of one. And you might be able to travel to see one. Some communities host eclipse parties when they are in the eclipse's path. They gather in backyards, schools, parks, campgrounds, beaches, and stadiums. And almost everyone can watch an eclipse over live streams on their computers or television.

Through experiments and observations, scientists learn more about the sun, the moon, and the earth itself by watching solar eclipses. Nonscientists come together to wonder about space and to try to observe all the fascinating ways the solar system moves, too. Solar eclipses are a thrill to see.

CHAPTER 1
History of Eclipses

Thousands of years ago, people wondered about many things they saw in the sky. They did not have telescopes, spacecraft, or other technologies that we have today. They could not use science to explain what they saw. They used stories instead.

The sun is important for life. It gives light and heat. It helps plants grow. Imagine how scary it would have been if the sun suddenly seemed to disappear! All over the world, ancient cultures created legends to explain eclipses. They told of monsters stealing the sun's light. In ancient Chinese stories, a dragon devoured the sun. In India, the demon Rahu swallowed it. Egyptians thought that a serpent from the

Nile River leaped into the sky and swallowed their sun god, Ra. There are stories that describe wolves, birds, bears, and other creatures eating the sun. To scare these enemies away, people made noise by yelling and banging on drums.

Rahu

They shot arrows and threw stones into the sky. Today, we know that eclipses are caused by the way the sun, earth, and moon move. But in the past, people saw eclipses as dangerous, and they worried for their lives.

Some cultures thought that eclipses were punishment from their gods. They thought the fog, dew, or rain after an eclipse would bring sickness. So they covered their wells, stayed inside, and did not drink water for days. During a battle between two kingdoms, near what is now Turkey, an eclipse darkened the sky. The soldiers put down their weapons, and the kings signed a treaty to end the war. To them, the eclipse seemed to be far more of a threat than any amount of fighting.

Other cultures had more romantic ideas. In Germany, they believed that the sun and the moon were married. Since the sun came out during the day, and the moon at night, the eclipse was the only time they could be together.

Early astronomers tried to understand more about the moon and sun. About five thousand years ago, people built stone structures related to the objects they saw in the sky. Stonehenge is an arrangement of giant rocks in England. The stones are lined up to mark the movements of the sun and the moon. Another collection of large stones in Ireland, called Loughcrew Cairns, are carved with circle shapes that might be symbols of a solar eclipse. These early structures show that people were noticing patterns in the way the sun and moon traveled across the sky.

As ancient astronomers learned more about the sky and watched the way objects moved over periods of time, they could predict when eclipses would occur. The Babylonians wrote records of eclipses on clay tablets almost four thousand years ago. They noticed that eclipses seemed to happen during certain times of the year, and that they repeated every eighteen years. Ancient Greek, Chinese, and Maya people also recorded and predicted eclipses.

Stonehenge

Recording Eclipses Through History

Scientists use computers to help them study eclipses and store information about them. But people all over the world have been recording information about eclipses for thousands of years, even before computers existed.

The earliest records of eclipses were pictures carved into rock, like the ones at Loughcrew Cairns in Ireland. These pictures are called petroglyphs. A petroglyph of a possible eclipse has also been found in New Mexico's Chaco Canyon.

In ancient China, observers wrote about eclipses by carving on animal bones. The Greeks wrote on long scrolls made from the papyrus plant. They also created a machine with bronze gears that helped them predict future positions of the sun and moon.

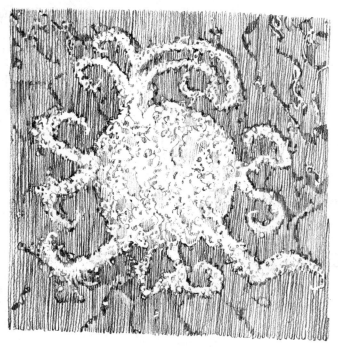

Chaco Canyon petroglyph

In Central America in the 1200s, the Maya wrote about eclipses in books made of tree fiber. These early astronomers recorded lots of information and predicted future eclipses. They even predicted an eclipse that happened more than seven hundred years later!

Over the centuries, astronomers continued to observe. They learned more about the sun, the moon, the earth, and the rest of the planets in our solar system. The invention of the telescope helped make faraway objects appear closer. Scientists developed spacecraft, called probes, to investigate the moon and the sun. High-powered cameras were designed to take photographs in different types of light. Modern tools like these have taught us a lot about our universe and our solar system, including eclipses.

CHAPTER 2
All About the Sun

We live in the Milky Way galaxy, a pinwheel-shaped collection of stars. The sun is one of these billions of stars. Some stars have planets that orbit, or move in a path, around them. Our sun has eight large planets that orbit it. These are Mercury, Venus, Earth, Mars, Jupiter, Saturn, Uranus, and Neptune. Smaller planets, rocks called asteroids, and chunks of dust and ice called comets also orbit the sun. The sun and all these objects make up our solar system.

Gravity is the pull of one object on another. The sun is the largest object in our solar system. It is more than one hundred times the size of earth. Because it is so large, it has lots of gravitational pull. The gravity keeps the planets and other space objects in orbit around it.

The sun doesn't have a hard surface like earth.

It is made up of the gases hydrogen and helium. Hydrogen burns in the center of the sun. It then turns into helium, which gives off light and heat. The temperature in the sun's center can reach more than twenty-seven million degrees!

The photosphere is the part of the sun that people on earth see as a circle in the sky. It is cooler than the center. But it is the brightest part of the sun. Next comes a reddish layer called the chromosphere. Sometimes hot gases shoot out from the chromosphere. The final layer is the corona. The corona is the outer atmosphere of the sun. It is a mixture of gases and particles that are always speeding away from the sun. This creates a solar wind that spreads out into the whole solar system. People can't often see the chromosphere or corona because the photosphere is so bright.

The sun is about ninety-three million miles

from earth. Earth is the third planet from the sun. Life doesn't exist on the other planets. Some are too close to the sun, others too far away. Earth is just right. The sun is the source of that power (both heat and light) that supports plants, animals, and people.

It takes earth one year to orbit the sun. The earth is tilted as it orbits. This tilt causes seasons on earth. When the top half of earth is tilted closer to the sun, it has summer, and the bottom half of the earth has winter. When the bottom half is tilted closer, it has summer, and the top half has winter.

From earth, the sun seems to rise and set in the sky. That's because the earth is always rotating, or spinning, on its axis. The sun shines on only half of the earth at a time. It takes about twenty-four hours for the earth to make one full turn. It is daytime on the side facing the sun. The other half of earth facing away is in shadow and has night.

Night

SUMMER

WINTER

Equator

Day

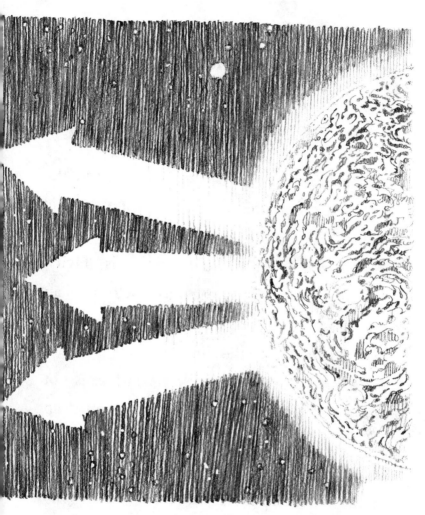

As the planet spins, the sun seems to travel across the sky during the day and disappear at night for those viewing it from earth.

CHAPTER 3
Space Partners

Earth has a partner in its orbit around the sun: its moon. The earth and moon travel together. The sun has gravity that keeps the earth in orbit around it. The earth has gravity, too. This gravity keeps the moon close in an oval-shaped path. So the moon orbits earth while the earth orbits the sun.

The moon is made of rock. Its surface is not smooth. It has flat plains, high hills, and deep valleys. Craters dot the surface. These round holes are left over from exploded volcanoes or spots where space rocks crashed into the moon.

One orbit of the moon around the earth takes a month. And because the orbit is oval shaped, sometimes the moon is closer to the earth and sometimes it is farther away. Just like the earth spins on an axis, so does the moon. It completes a spin once each month. That means that the same side of the moon is always facing earth.

The moon seems to glow, but it does not give off its own light. People on earth see the sun's light being reflected by, or bouncing off, the moon's surface. The side of the moon facing the sun looks bright, and the other half looks dark because it is in shadow. Because of the way the moon orbits the earth, we don't always see all of the moon's bright side over a month's time. The different amounts of the moon's bright surface we can see are the moon's phases.

During a new moon, the side of the moon in shadow faces earth, so we can't see the moon in the sky. Next comes a waxing crescent,

then the first quarter, then a waxing gibbous. *Waxing* means getting bigger. The halfway point of the phases is called the full moon.

That's when the moon looks like a full bright circle in the sky. This is the bright side of the moon.

After a full moon, the moon seems to grow smaller. It becomes a waning gibbous, then the last quarter, and a waning crescent. *Waning* means getting smaller. Finally, the moon seems to disappear when it is in its new moon phase. The shadowed side of the moon faces the earth again.

The moon is in the sky during the day. But

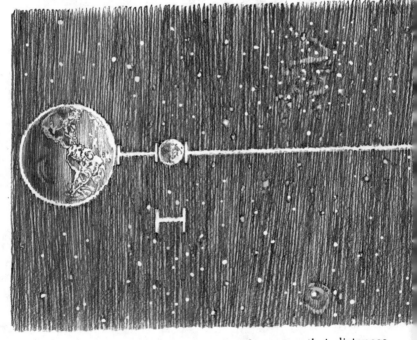

Comparison of the width of the sun and moon vs. their distances from earth (not to scale)

the sun's light is so bright that it makes it harder to find. The sun and the moon look like they are about the same size. But the sun is actually about four hundred times wider than the moon. They appear the same because of their distances from earth. The sun is about four hundred times farther away from earth than the moon. So they look the same size when we gaze at the sky.

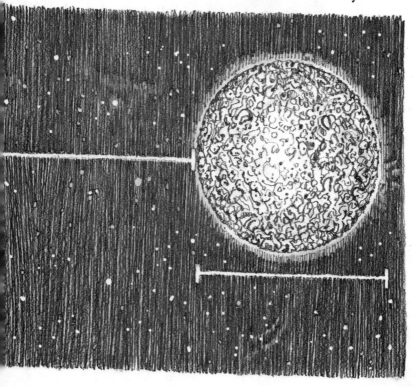

CHAPTER 4
In the Way!

A solar eclipse happens during the day when the sun, moon, and earth are all lined up within their orbits. The moon moves between the sun and the earth, blocking the sun's light and casting a dark shadow on the earth's surface.

It might seem that an eclipse could happen every month during a new moon when the sun is shining on the side of the moon facing away from earth. But the orbits of the earth around the sun and the moon around the earth are not in the same flat plane. They are tilted. So the shadow created by the moon doesn't always hit the earth. Only about twice a year, during eclipse seasons, are the orbits likely to be lined up in the right way for the moon's shadow to pass over earth.

Types of Eclipses

There are three types of solar eclipses: total, annular, and partial.

During a *total solar eclipse*, the circle of the moon in the sky completely blocks the circle of the sun. The sun's corona can be seen, and the shadow on earth makes day seem like night.

An *annular solar eclipse* happens when the circle of the moon lines up over the circle of the sun, but the moon doesn't completely cover the face of the sun. This happens when the moon is at the point in its orbit when it is the farthest from earth. The moon still blocks most of the sun's light, but we can still see a ring of sunlight around the edge. It appears as if the moon is just a little bit smaller than the sun.

During a *partial solar eclipse*, the sun, moon, and earth are close to, but not quite, lined up.

The moon blocks part of the sun's light but does not pass directly in front of it. The sun appears as a crescent shape in the sky.

There are also *lunar eclipses*, which happen at night. During a lunar eclipse, the earth gets between the sun and the moon. The earth's shadow crosses over the moon's surface. This happens at the full moon phase, but the moon appears red in the sky. That's because the sun's light is passing through the atmosphere of the earth before it reaches the moon.

Even though solar eclipses happen frequently, they are not always easy for people to view. The paths cross areas that do not have large populations. The earth is covered with a lot more water than land, so the path of an eclipse often passes over the ocean. An eclipse might pass over the very top or bottom of earth, the two areas called its poles. The weather at the poles is extremely cold, so few people live there.

Total solar eclipses last about three hours. Because the earth is spinning, the shadow cast by the eclipse moves in a diagonal path across about one-third of earth's surface. The shadow has two parts.

The umbra is the darkest, inner part of the shadow where light is completely blocked. It is about seventy miles wide. In the umbra, viewers on earth will see a total eclipse. This is called the path of totality. The penumbra is the outer edge of the shadow where there is still some light. In the penumbra path (about three hundred miles wide), viewers will see a partial eclipse.

CHAPTER 5
The View from Earth

If the weather is clear in the path of totality, sky watchers are in for quite a sight! Scientists have divided the steps of a total solar eclipse into first contact, second contact, totality, third contact, and fourth contact. Through all the steps, except for totality, people *must* wear special filtered glasses to watch an eclipse. First contact happens when the circle of the moon appears to touch the outer circle of the sun. Then it appears to cross over the sun's surface. The sun becomes a crescent shape. First it will look like a cookie with a bite taken out of the edge. Over the next hour or so, the crescent will get thinner and thinner.

Less of the sun's light reaches earth, so the daylight starts to look a bit strange. Shadows get sharper. The temperature drops. Animals act confused. They rely on the light from the sun to know the difference between night and day. They think night is coming. Birds may stop

singing and head toward their nests. Nocturnal animals that come out only at night, like bats and owls, sometimes start to stir. Farm animals may head back to their barns.

Shadow bands appear on the ground or sides of buildings. These are twinkling ripples of light and shadow. Scientists are not sure what causes shadow bands, but they believe these light waves are likely an effect caused by the sun's changing light shining through the gases of earth's atmosphere.

If the sun is shining through leaves on a tree, the shadows on the ground will look crescent shaped. If you spread out your fingers and place one hand on top of the other, you can make these shadows, too. Hold your hands so the sun shines through them, and you may see crescent-shaped shadows on the ground.

When the sun is just a thin sliver, you may see Baily's beads. These small points of light last only a second! They are caused by the sunlight shining through the valleys on the moon's surface. The moon's bumpy surface may also cause what is called "the diamond ring"— a brief bright point of light shining through a deep canyon on the moon.

Second contact is the moment that the moon completely covers the sun. Totality has begun. This is the only time it is safe to take off viewing glasses. Without the bright light of the photosphere, the day becomes as dark as night. The sun's corona appears like a feathery halo of light around a dark center. The thin reddish ring of the chromosphere may also be visible at the base of the corona. In the dark sky around the sun, stars and planets that are never visible in the daytime now appear.

Totality lasts a few minutes. Viewing glasses must be worn again before third contact—the moment the moon starts moving from in front of the sun. The crescent of the sun appears to grow larger until the moon looks as if it's just touching the edge of the sun. This is fourth contact. Then the moon no longer blocks the sun's light. The eclipse is over. The whole process takes about three to four hours.

Safety First!

It is amazing to watch a solar eclipse, but it is not safe for your eyes. The sun is so bright that you can burn your retina, the part of your eye that takes in light. And looking at the sun through a camera, binoculars, or a telescope makes the sun's rays even more intense. If you look directly at the sun for any length of time, you will damage your eyes.

You can look at the sun with special solar eclipse glasses. These are not regular sunglasses. They are made specifically for eclipse viewing, with approved filters that block out the harmful rays of the sun.

The only time it is safe to look directly at an eclipse is when it is in totality and the circle of the moon is completely covering the photosphere of the sun. You can take off your glasses at this time, but you must put them back on before totality ends.

You can also watch an eclipse without looking directly at it with a pinhole projector. All you need to make one is an index card and a piece of paper. Punch a hole in the index card. Place the paper flat on the ground. Then stand with your back to the sun and hold out the index card so that the sun's light shines through the hole and down onto the paper. You will see the changing shape of the sun on the paper.

Scientists have learned a lot by studying eclipses. They learned how the sun, earth, and moon move. And computer models have helped them accurately predict eclipses. Space organizations all over the world work together to share information and watch eclipses from different points of view. The International Space Station, a laboratory orbiting the earth, sends back data from space. Scientists sometimes get help collecting data from citizen scientists. A citizen scientist is a person (not a trained scientist) who records what they see and sends the information to space organizations. This is fun for the citizen scientist and helpful to the professional scientists. The more data the organization receives, the more they can learn about eclipses. You could be a citizen scientist, too! Tools, technology, and people working together help everyone learn more about eclipses. There are always new ideas to test and discover.

The cycle of eclipses promises there will always be more total solar eclipses to view. Almost seventy will happen in this century. Eclipse maps show where and when they will happen. Perhaps you can travel to see an eclipse. Maybe one will pass right over your town or city. Wear eclipse glasses, look to the sky, and see the solar system in motion!

The View from Space

We know what an eclipse looks like in the sky from our point of view on earth. But what would a solar eclipse look like from space?

The International Space Station (ISS) is a spacecraft that orbits earth. Astronauts from several countries live and work there. They do experiments and study to learn more about travel in space. From that view high above, astronauts also have been able to observe solar eclipses.

An astronaut on the ISS can see the shadow of the moon on the earth's surface. It looks like a circle or oval. They can observe the darkest umbra in the center of the shadow, and the fuzzy penumbra around it. On earth, the areas of land or ocean under the umbra are experiencing a total eclipse. Those under the penumbra are seeing a partial eclipse.

You don't have to be an astronaut to see what an eclipse would look like from high above. Satellites orbiting around earth also send back pictures during an eclipse. We can get a space view without ever leaving the ground!

The moon's shadow during a solar eclipse, as seen from the ISS

Timeline of Solar Eclipses

3340 BC — Loughcrew Cairns are carved with the first recorded image of an eclipse

3000 BC–2500 BC — Stonehenge is built

1700 BC — The first found Babylonian record of eclipses

772 BC–481 BC — Ancient Chinese astronomers record accounts of eclipses and start to predict them

585 BC — On May 28, soldiers fighting near present-day Turkey see an eclipse, drop their weapons, and call for peace

AD 1133 — King Henry's Eclipse happens August 2

1836 — English astronomer Francis Baily explains the appearance of points of light during an eclipse

1851 — Johann Julius Friedrich Berkowski takes the first successful photograph of the sun's corona

1878 — The path of a solar eclipse passes over the American West

1919 — An eclipse helps prove Albert Einstein's theory that heavy objects like the sun can bend light

2017 — On August 21, the path of totality of the Great American Total Solar Eclipse crosses the United States from Oregon to South Carolina

2024 — The path of totality of the April 8 eclipse passes over Mexico, the United States, and Canada

Timeline of the World

bya = billion years ago, mya = million years ago

4.5 bya	The solar system forms
65 mya	An asteroid hits earth and causes huge dust clouds that kill off the dinosaurs and other large animals
c. 600 BC	Greek philosopher Anaximander creates the first map of the world
AD 1519– 1522	Portuguese explorer Ferdinand Magellan's expedition successfully sails around the globe
1543	Polish astronomer Copernicus first suggests that the sun is the center of the solar system, not the earth
1609	Italian astronomer Galileo uses the telescope to study objects in space
1687	English mathematician and astronomer Isaac Newton explains his law of gravity
1798	German astronomer Caroline Herschel studies comets, and her findings are the first written by a woman to be read at the Royal Society in England
1969	NASA sends astronauts to land on the moon during the Apollo 11 mission
1998–2011	Many countries contribute to the building of the International Space Station
2018	NASA launches the Parker Solar Probe to orbit the sun and fly through its corona

Bibliography

*Books for young readers

AAS Solar Eclipse Task Force. "How to View a Solar Eclipse Safely." American Astronomical Society. https://eclipse.aas.org/ eye-safety.

"Eclipse." Almanac.com. https://www.almanac.com/topics/ astronomy/eclipse.

*Gifford, Clive. *Super Space Encyclopedia*. New York: DK Publishing, 2019.

Littmann, Mark, and Fred Espenak. *Totality: The Great American Eclipses of 2017 and 2024*. Oxford: Oxford University Press, 2017.

Mansky, Jackie. "A Brief History of Eclipse Chasers." *Smithsonian Magazine*, August 3, 2017. https://www.smithsonianmag. com/travel/brief-history-eclipse-chasers-180964063/.

NASA Goddard's Solar System Exploration Division. "Moon in Motion." NASA Science. https://moon.nasa.gov/moon-in-motion/overview/.

North, Chris, and Paul Abel. *How to Read the Solar System: A Guide to the Stars and Planets*. New York: Pegasus Books, 2014.

St. Fleur, Nicholas. "An Eclipse Chaser's Guide to Your First Eclipse." *New York Times*, August 14, 2017. https://www.nytimes.com/2017/08/14/science/eclipse-chasers-first.html.

Zeiler, Michael. "2 Great American Eclipses." GreatAmericanEclipse.com. https://www.greatamericaneclipse.com/.

Websites

earthsky.org
eclipse2017.nasa.gov/eclipse-101
kidseclipse.com
solarsystem.nasa.gov